September

2023

MESSIANIC CALENDAR

Contains All Jewish Feast Explanations

YahShuah Ben Yahweh

Publication

1

SHABBAT

pronounced Sha-baht, begins every Friday Eve and lasts 25 hours. It is a day to celebrate with the Lord, while resting and enjoying family. Shabbat begins with the lighting of candles and if you're having a Shabbat dinner to mark the separation of time from the week that is coming to an end, it will include a blessing of the food and drink accompanied by a candle lighting ceremony.

Many individuals celebrate Shabbat in different ways. Some people don't spend money, some turn off their phone over dinner, others go to synagogue services, and some observe strict rules regarding studying Torah.

The end of Shabbat is traditionally marked by a ritual called Havdalah during which songs are sung and blessings are said over wine/grape juice, spices, and light (a special twisted candle is used), separating Shabbat from the rest of the week.

Tu Bishvat, The New Year for Trees

or 15th day of Hebrew month of Shvat

When the Temple in Jerusalem was still standing, Jews offered the first fruits of their trees on Tu Bishvat. You could call it the birthday of the trees and it is now thought of as an environmental holiday.

Jewish Holiday Foods include fruit, nuts and other things that grow on or in trees, including the seven species mentioned in the Torah: wheat, barley, grapes, figs, pomegranates, olives, and dates.

Activities include a ritual meal as an opportunity to explore environmental themes in Judaism. Another practice is to plant trees. This is a minor festival in that there is no obligation not to work.

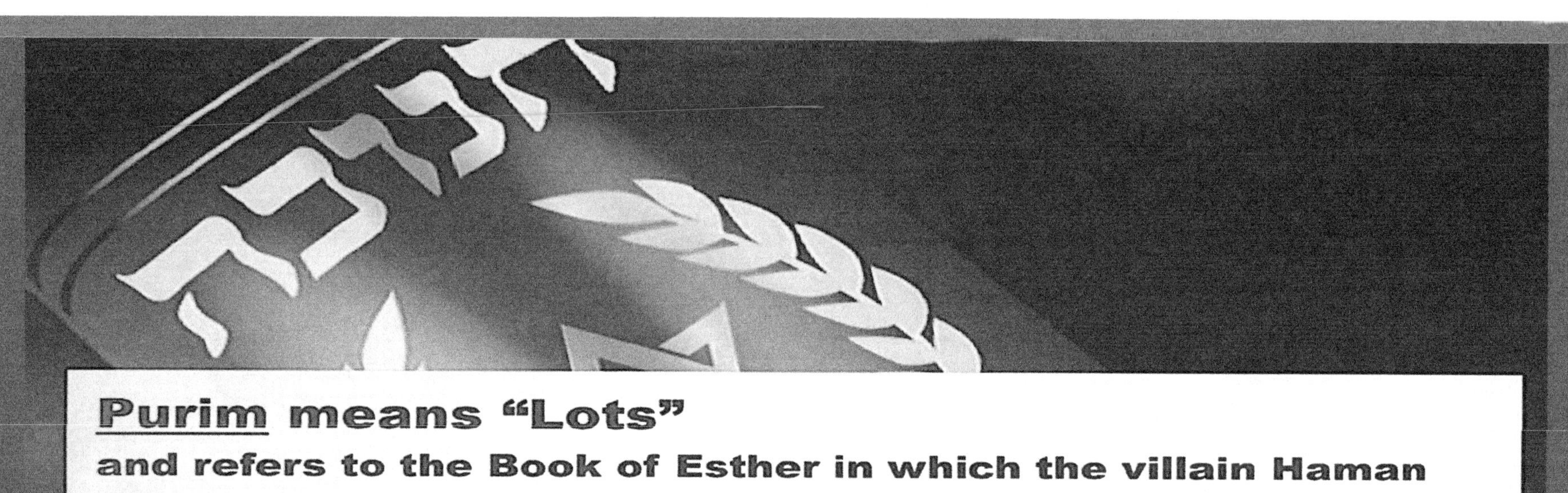

Purim means “Lots”

and refers to the Book of Esther in which the villain Haman draws lots to set the date for the Jews’ destruction.
Its about a celebration of the narrow escape from genocide of the Jews described in the biblical Book of Esther. On Purim we read the Book of Esther and use noisemakers (called graggers) to drown out the name of the evil Haman, who wanted to kill all of the Jewish children. Many adults get dressed up in costumes and eat triangular cookies and other treats.

Yom HaShoah means Holocaust Day

Europeans commemorate the Holocaust on the anniversary of the liberation of Auschwitz, Jan. 27, 1945. The Israeli government, however, wanted a date that would honor Jewish resistance to the Nazi genocide of World War II.

After some debate, it was decided that Yom HaShoah would be observed on the 27th of the Hebrew month of Nisan, since it was during the period of the Warsaw Ghetto Uprising, an act of Jewish heroism and resistance.

In the United States, Yom Ha-Shoah is observed on the 27th of Nisaan. Many communities hold commemorative events and yahrzeit (annual memorial) candles are lit.

<u>Shavuot</u> means Feast of Weeks

Shavuot is celebrated seven weeks after Passover and combines two ancient holidays: The giving of Torah at Mt. Sinai that marks the covenant between God and the Jewish people (seven weeks after the Exodus from Egypt) and the Early Summer Grain Harvest. It's traditional to eat dairy food Shavuot, so lots of blintzes, cheese and ice cream. (On "dair holidays" people who keep kosher do not eat meat.)

The Book of Ruth (a story about interfaith marriage and family.) It is read in synagogues during the feast and some people participate in an all-night Torah study session called Tikkun Leil Shavuot.

Passover (Pesach) means "Pass over"

This 8-day holiday (though some celebrate 7 days) commemorates God freeing the Israelites from slavery in Egypt. The name refers to God "passing over" the houses of the Israelites during the 10th plague, (the killing of the first born.)

Traditionally, Jews eat no bread or leavened food on Passover, and instead eat matzah, which is unleavened bread. There are many traditional foods that are eaten on Passover, including matzah balls, gefilte fish and macaroons. Additionally, there are many symbolic foods that appear on the seder plate that are explained during the seder.

Activities include Spring cleaning and seders. Seders are heavily ritualized holiday meals in which we are commanded to tell the story of Passover every year. Passover is the most celebrated Jewish holiday is the world and different Jewish cultures have different food and rituals.

Tisha B'Av

Tisha B'Av means Ninth day of the Hebrew month of Av

This is the saddest day in the Jewish calendar. This fast day commemorates the Roman destruction of the Second Temple. In the medieval period, Jews began attaching other tragedies to the day, including the expulsion from Spain in 1492, making it a general day of mourning.Though this is a major fast day with no food, water or washing, it is a minor holiday in the sense that there is no requirement to abstain from work. One unusual feature of Tisha B'Av is that it's traditional not to greet people during the fast. This comes from Jewish mourning practices.

Tu B'Av

In ancient times on Tu B'Av (literally the 15th of the month of Av), when the moon is full, women wishing to marry would wear white dresses (so none would know who was rich or poor) and dance outside Jerusalem's walls while suitors would dance after them. Today in the Jewish world, it is a holiday celebrating the magic of love.

Lag B'Omer literally means the 33rd day of the Omer. This day is derived from the practice of counting the Omer or the days from the barley offering at the temple to the day of the wheat offering on Shavout.

TA' ANIT ESTHER is not an official observant day but has been adopted by most.

It commemorates the fasting of our ancestors in response to the dramatic chain of events that occurred during their exile in the Persian empire.

It is a universal aspect of the human condition that time marches on. Jewish tradition seeks not only to mark the passage of time, but to make it holy. In the fall, Jewish communities the world over observe what is known in Hebrew as *Hayamim Hanoraim* (the Days of Awe). This 10-day period opens with **Rosh Hashanah** (Jewish New Year) celebrated for two days, and concludes with the one-day observance of **Yom Kippur** (Day of Atonement). The 10 days are a time for reflecting on the past year, making amends, and celebrating hope for the future. This year in particular, we as a community are leaning into hope individually and collectively, to help heal hearts, bodies, and the planet—and forge a united, inclusive path forward.

Sukkot means, Booths or Tabernacles

In ancient times when the Temple stood in Jerusalem, this was a pilgrimage holiday to celebrate the harvest. Rabbinic tradition now holds that this week-long holiday is when we remember the experience of the Israelite's years of wandering in the desert. Pronounce it: Sue-coat.

Families and communities build a sukkah (or hut) in the yard that will be used for the whole week of Sukkot for eating and entertaining. Some people even sleep in their sukkah.

These huts remind us of the ones our ancestors dwelled in while wandering in the desert. The sukkah should have 3 sides and a roof, but still be open to the elements. The sukkah, the lulav (a palm frond) and the etrog (a kind of citrus) that are used in the ritual to celebrate bounty. Hag Sameah or Gut Yonif (Happy holiday, in Hebrew and Yiddish, respectively) is the proper greeting for the first and last days of holiday, whereas the proper greeting for the intermediate days is Moadim l'simcha, which means "festivals for joy."

Yom Kippur means: Day of Atonement

Or a fast day that is traditionally filled with prayer and collective confession and atonement.

This is a fast day for those not exempt from fasting. Many people go to synagogue for most of the day, and even those who are not observant may go for a special service called Yizkor, that honors the dead. The fast (and holiday) ends with a festive break-fast meal after sundown.

Simchat Torah means Rejoicing in the Torah

It celebrates the end of reading of the year's Torah cycle and starting it anew for the new year. On this holiday, we finish the annual cycle of Torah reading, and read the very last words of the Torah. As soon as we finish the Torah, we start reading it over from the beginning. The service is punctuated by the congregation dancing with the Torah scrolls.

Chanukah or The Feast Of Dedication

This holiday is an 8-day holiday that commemorates the Jewish recapture and rededication of the Temple in Jerusalem in 164 BCE.

Chanukah is noted by the enjoyment of eating fried foods, especially potato pancakes, called latkes, and jelly doughnuts called Sufganiyot. We eat foods fried in oil to remind us of the small amount of oil (just enough for one day) that miraculously burned for eight days when the Jews rededicated the Temple. The main observance is lighting the candles in a ceremonial lamp called a Hanukkiah, or Hanukkah menorah, each night for all 8 nights.

Playing with a top called a Dreidel is another fun tradition. Hanukkah is a "minor festival" in the sense that there is no requirement to abstain from work.

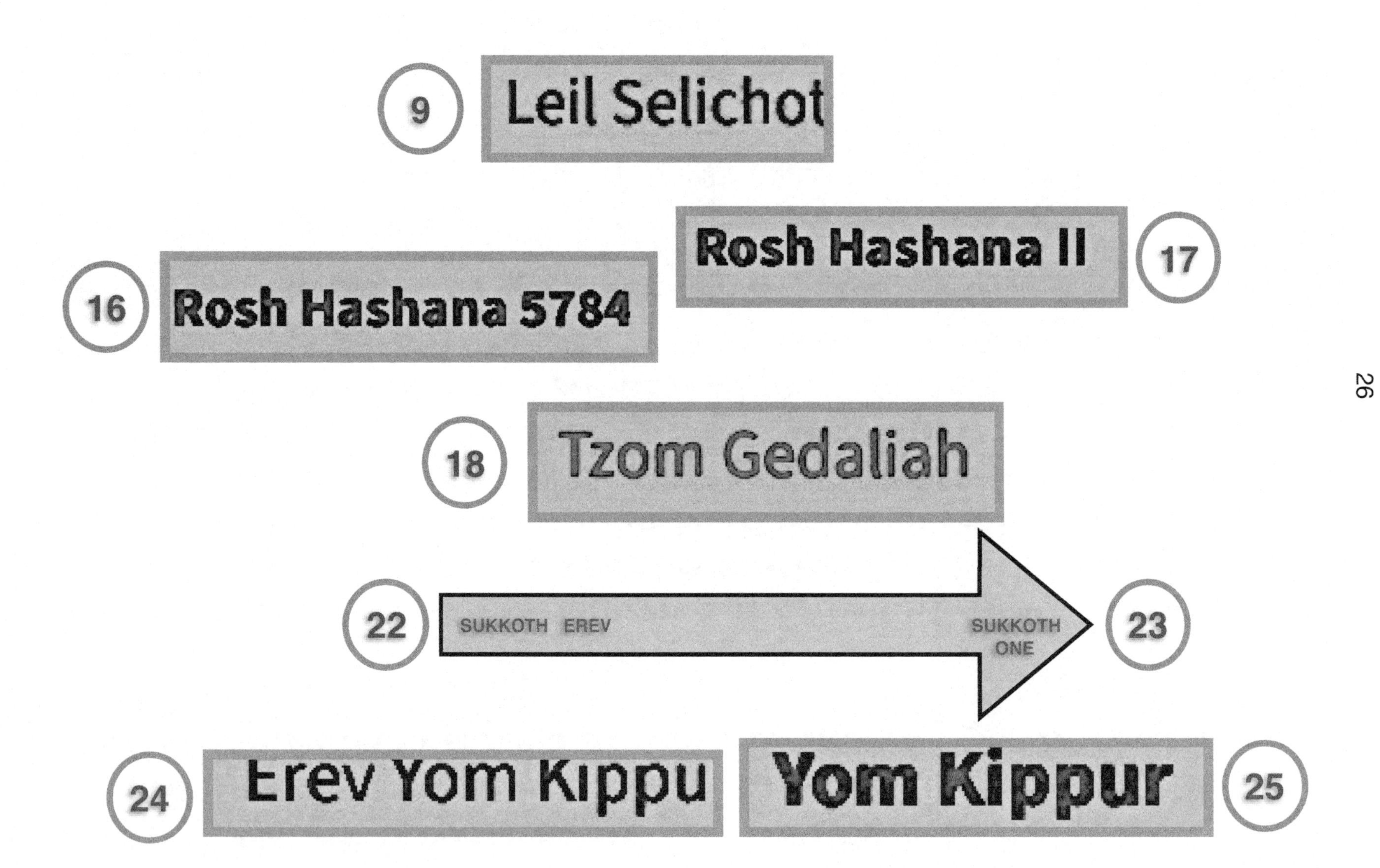
9
Leil Selichot
16
Rosh Hashana 5784
Rosh Hashana II
17
18
Tzom Gedaliah
22
SUKKOTH EREV
SUKKOTH ONE
23
24
Erev Yom Kippu
Yom Kippur
25

SEPTEMBER 2023

SUNDAY	MONDAY	TUESDAY	WEDNESDAY	THURSDAY	FRIDAY	SATURDAY
			YahshuahBenYahweh Publications		1	2
3	4	5	6	7	8	9 Leil Selichot
10	11	12	13	14	15	16 Rosh Hashana 5784
17 Rosh Hashana II	18 Tzom Gedaliah	19	20	21	22 SUKKOTH EREV	23 SUKKOTH ONE
24 Erev Yom Kippu	25 Yom Kippur	26	27	28	29	30

1
SUKKOTH
TWO
THREE
FOUR
FIVE
SIX
SEVEN
6
7
Shmini Atzeret
8
Simchat Torah
YahshuahBenYahweh
Publications

OCTOBER 2023

SUNDAY	MONDAY	TUESDAY	WEDNESDAY	THURSDAY	FRIDAY	SATURDAY
1	2	3	4	5	6	7
SUKKOTH	TWO	THREE	FOUR	FIVE	SIX	Shmini Atzeret
8 Simchat Torah	9	10	11	12	13	14
15	16	17	18	19	20	21
22	23	24	25	26	27	28
29	30	31				

13 Sigd

Rosh Chodesh Kislev 14

NOVEMBER 2023

SUNDAY	MONDAY	TUESDAY	WEDNESDAY	THURSDAY	FRIDAY	SATURDAY
			1	2	3	4
5	6	7	8	9	10	11
12	13 Sigd	14 Rosh Chodesh Kislev	15	16	17	18
19	20	21	22	23	24	25
26	27	28	29	30		

7

24th of Kislev

Chanukah: 1 Candle

Chanukah: 8th Day

15

22

Asara B'Tevet

DECEMBER 2023

SUNDAY	MONDAY	TUESDAY	WEDNESDAY	THURSDAY	FRIDAY	SATURDAY
					1	2
3	4	5	6	7 CHANUKAH CANDLE ONE	8 CHANUKAH CANDLE TWO	9 CHANUKAH CANDLE THREE
10 CHANUKAH CANDLE FOUR	11 CHANUKAH CANDLE FIVE	12 CHANUKAH CANDLE SIX	13 CHANUKAH CANDLE SEVEN	14 CHANUKAH CANDLE EIGHT	15 Chanukah: 8th Day	16
17	18	19	20	21	22 Asara B'Tevet	23
24	25	26	27	28	29	30
31						

11 Rosh Chodesh Sh'vat

25 Tu BiShvat

27

JANUARY 2024

SUNDAY	MONDAY	TUESDAY	WEDNESDAY	THURSDAY	FRIDAY	SATURDAY
YahshuahBenYahweh Publications	1	2	3	4	5	6
7	8	9	10	11 Rosh Chodesh Sh'vat	12	13
14	15	16	17	18	19	20
21	22	23	24	25 Tu BiShvat	26	27 Shabbat Shirah
28	29	30	31			

9 Rosh Chodesh Adar

Rosh Chodesh Adar

Purim Katan

FEBRUARY 2024

SUNDAY	MONDAY	TUESDAY	WEDNESDAY	THURSDAY	FRIDAY	SATURDAY
				1	2	3
4	5	6	7	8	9 Rosh Chodesh Adar I	10 Rosh Chodesh Adar I
11	12	13	14	15	16	17
18	19	20	21	22	23 Purim Katan	24
25	26	27	28	29		

9 Shabbat Shekalim

10 Rosh Chodesh Adar

21 Ta'anit Esther

23 Shabbat Zachor
Erev Purim

24 Purim

25 Shushan Purim

30 Shabbat Parah

MARCH 2024

SUNDAY	MONDAY	TUESDAY	WEDNESDAY	THURSDAY	FRIDAY	SATURDAY
					1	2
3	4	5	6	7	8	9 Shabbat Shekalim
10 30th of Adar I Rosh Chodesh Adar II	11 1st of Adar II, 5784 Rosh Chodesh Adar II	12	13	14	15	16
17	18	19	20	21 Ta'anit Esther	22	23 Shabbat Zachor Erev Purim
24 Purim	25 Shushan Purim	26	27	28	29	30 Shabbat Parah
31						

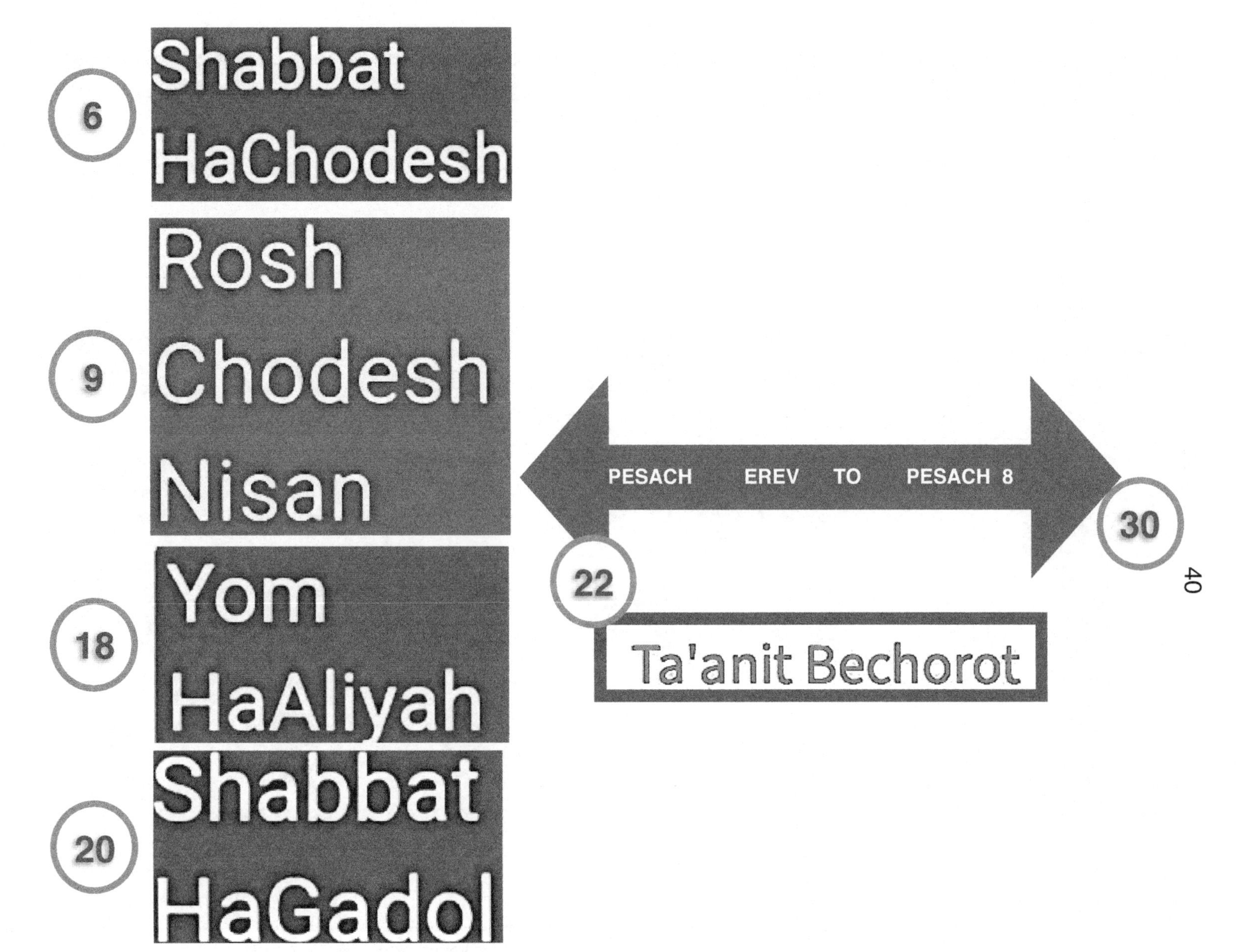
6
Shabbat HaChodesh
9
Rosh Chodesh Nisan
18
Yom HaAliyah
20
Shabbat HaGadol
PESACH EREV TO PESACH 8
22
30
Ta'anit Bechorot

APRIL 2024

SUNDAY	MONDAY	TUESDAY	WEDNESDAY	THURSDAY	FRIDAY	SATURDAY
	1	2	3	4	5	6 Shabbat HaChodesh
7	8	9 Rosh Chodesh Nisan	10	11	12	13
14	15	16	17	18 Yom HaAliyah	19	20 Shabbat HaGadol
21	22 Ta'anit Bechorot Erev Pesach	23	24	25	26	27 Pesach V (CH"M)
28	29	30				

PESACH SIX PESACH SEVEN PESACH EIGHT

6 Yom HaShoah

8 Rosh Chodesh Iyyar

9 Rosh Chodesh Iyyar

13 Yom HaZikaron

Yom HaAtzma'ut

Pesach Sheni

Lag BaOmer

MAY 2024

SUNDAY	MONDAY	TUESDAY	WEDNESDAY	THURSDAY	FRIDAY	SATURDAY
	YahshuahBenYahweh Publications		1	2	3	4
5	6 Yom HaShoah	7	8 Rosh Chodesh Iyyar	9 Rosh Chodesh Iyyar	10	11
12	13 Yom HaZikaron	14 Yom HaAtzma'ut	15	16	17	18
19	20	21	22 Pesach Sheni	23	24	25
26 Lag BaOmer	27	28	29	30	31	

5 Yom Yerushalayim

Rosh Chodesh Sivan 7

Erev

11 SHAVUOT TILL 13

JUNE 2024

SUNDAY	MONDAY	TUESDAY	WEDNESDAY	THURSDAY	FRIDAY	SATURDAY
						1
2	3	4	5 Yom Yerushalayim	6	7 Rosh Chodesh Sivan	8
9	10	Erev 11 Shavuot	12	13	14	15
16	17	18	19	20	21	22
23	24	25	26	27	28	29
30						

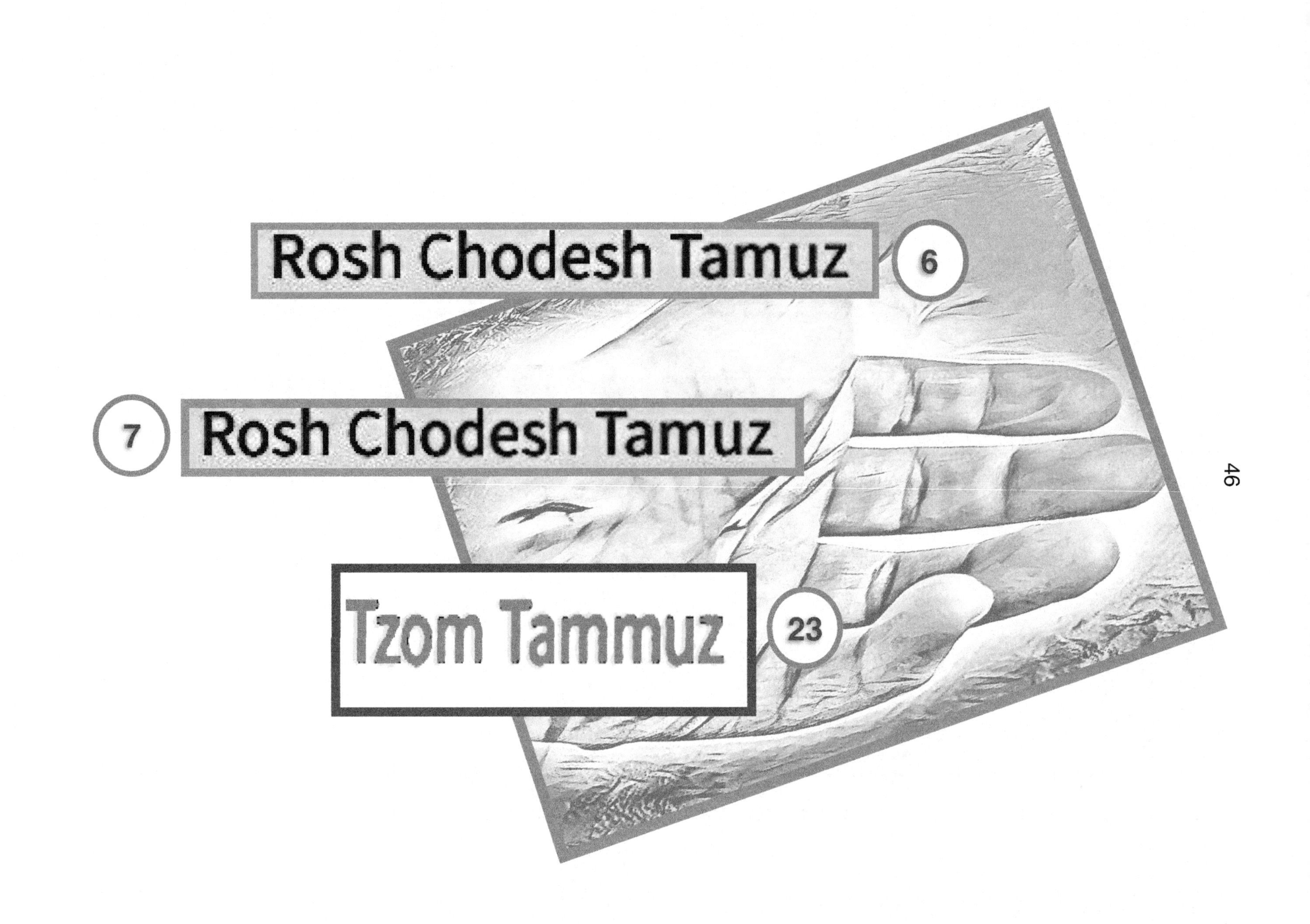
Rosh Chodesh Tamuz
6
7
Rosh Chodesh Tamuz
Tzom Tammuz
23

JULY 2024

SUNDAY	MONDAY	TUESDAY	WEDNESDAY	THURSDAY	FRIDAY	SATURDAY
	1	2	3	4	5	6 Rosh Chodesh Tamuz
7 Rosh Chodesh Tamuz	8	9	10	11	12	13
14	15	16	17	18	19	20
21	22	23 Tzom Tammuz	24	25	26	27
28	29	30	31			

Shabbat Chazon 10

12 Erev Tish'a B'Av

13 Tish'a B'Av

Shabbat Nachamu 17

19 Tu B'Av

AUGUST 2024

SUNDAY	MONDAY	TUESDAY	WEDNESDAY	THURSDAY	FRIDAY	SATURDAY
			YahshuahBenYahweh Publications	1	2	3
4	5	6	7	8	9	10 Shabbat Chazon
11	12 Erev Tish'a B'Av	13 Tish'a B'Av	14	15	16	17 Shabbat Nachamu
18	19 Tu B'Av	20	21	22	23	24
25	26	27	28	29	30	31

Printed in Great Britain
by Amazon